Super Fun Activity Workbook

Sulaiha Shameena

Copyright

Made with ❤ on the Notion Press Platform
www.notionpress.com

Trace the patterns

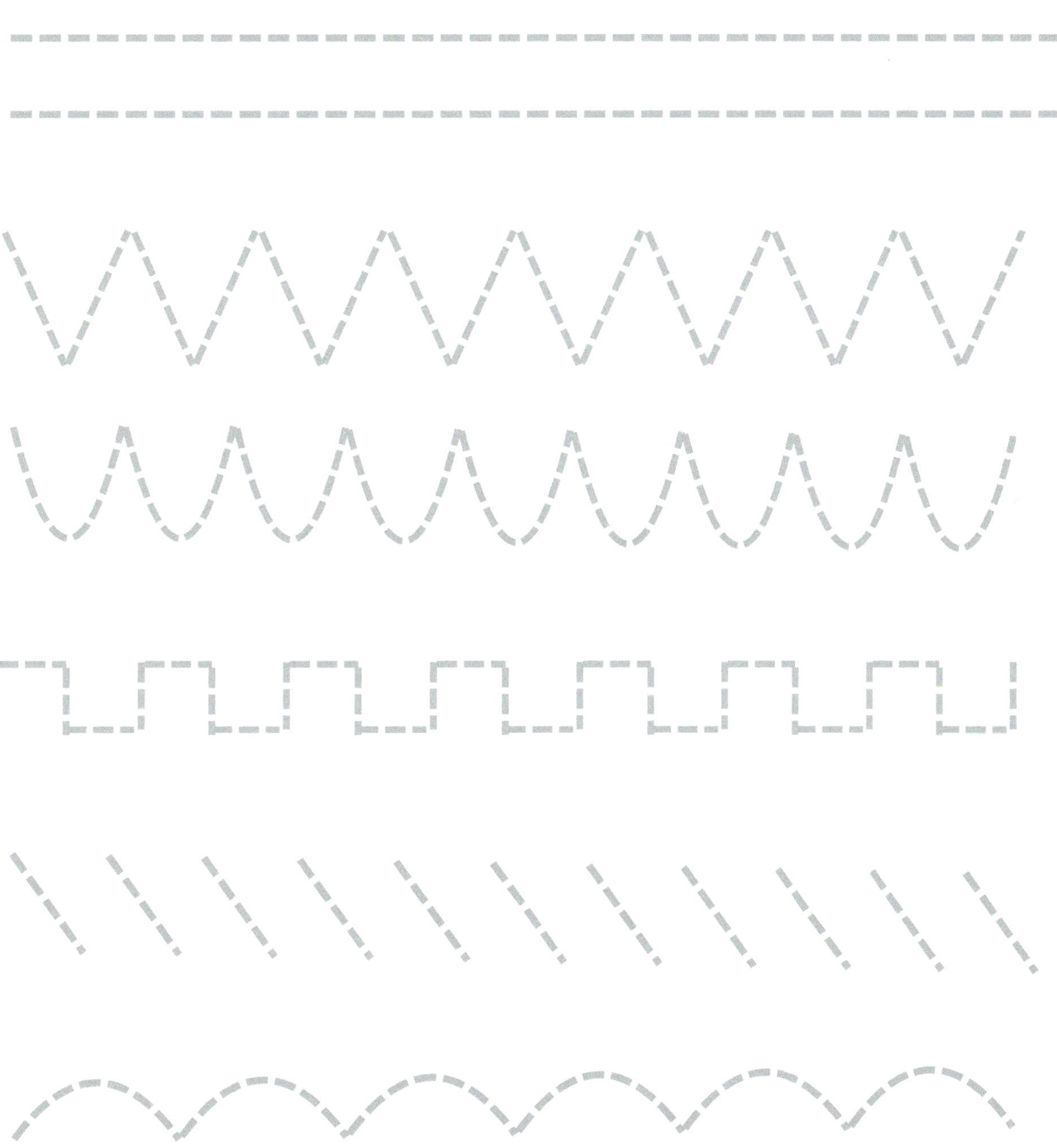

Trace the shapes

Trace the picture

Circle the object as per the number given

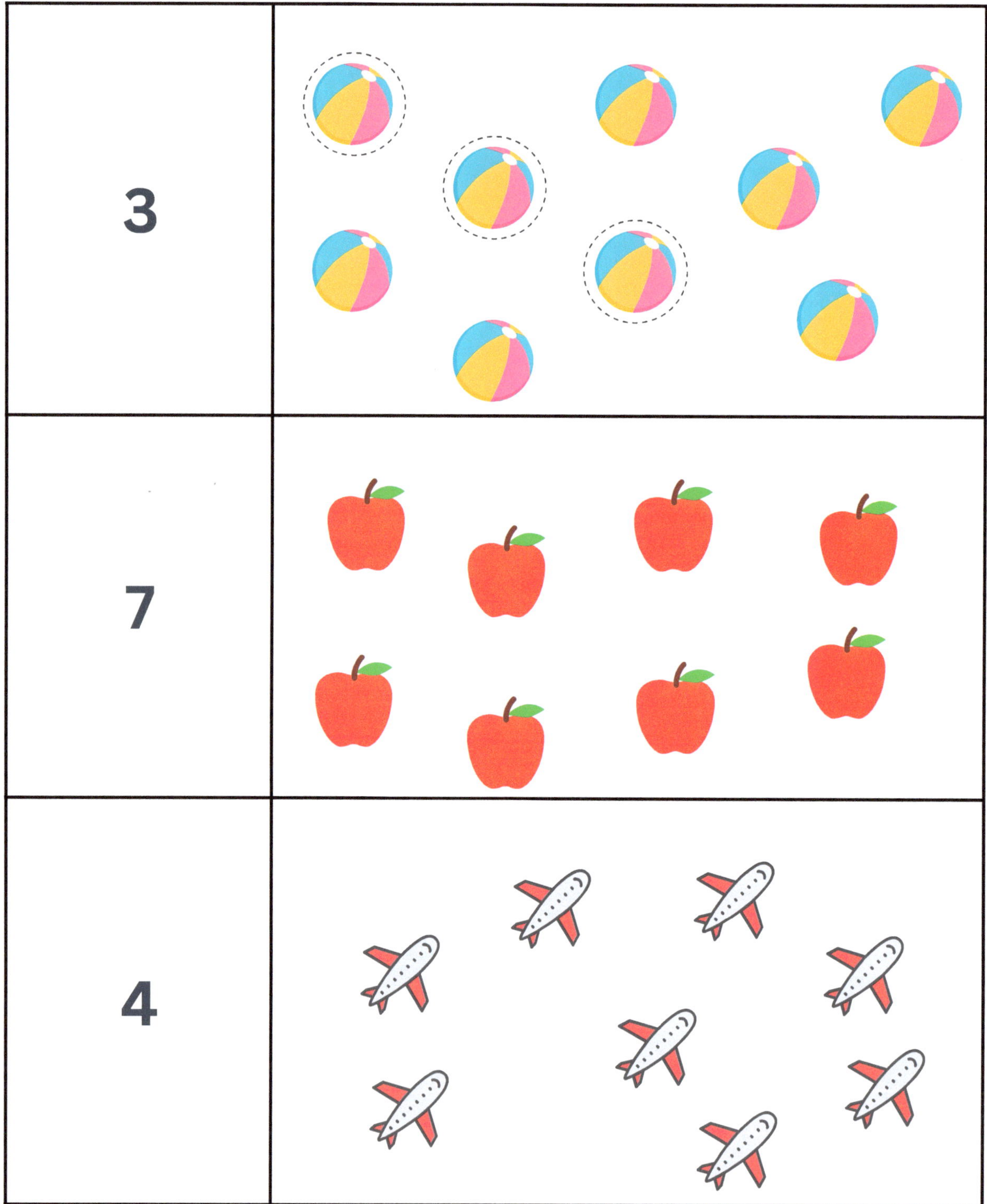

Circle the object as per the number given

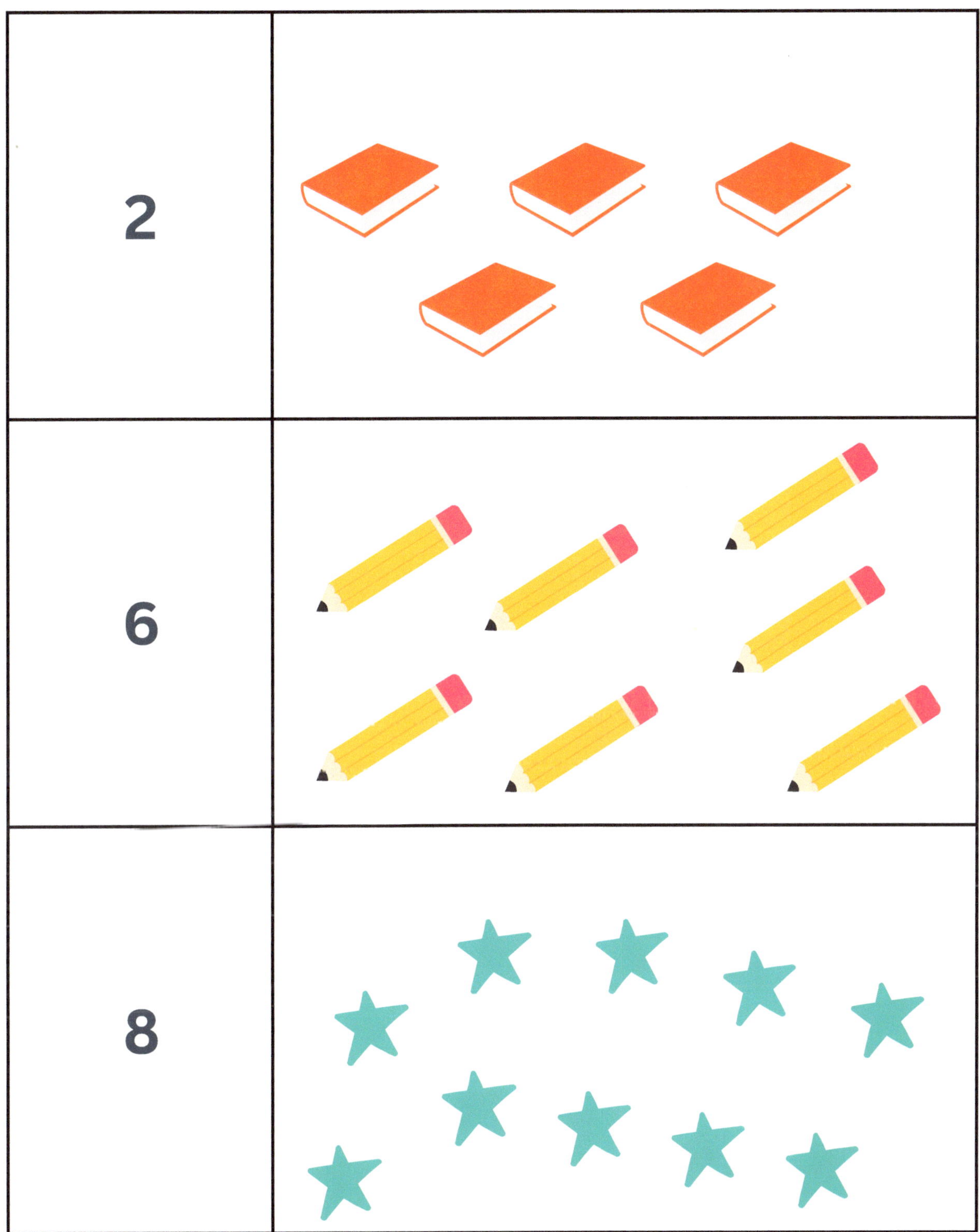

Match the words with the pictures

Lion 

Cat 

Dog 

Zebra 

Camel 

Match the words with the pictures

Peacock

Penquin

Crow

Eagle

Duck

Match the words with the pictures

Happy

Sad

Surprised

Scared

Crying

Match the words with the pictures

Cycle	
Car	
Scooter	
Airplane	
Train	

Match the words with the pictures

Root

Stem

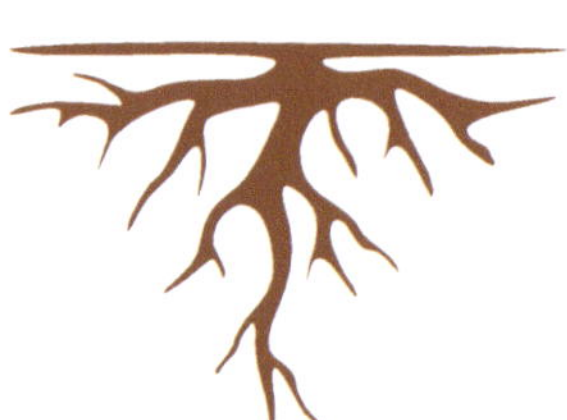

Leaf

Fruit

Flower

Match the words with the pictures

Police

Doctor

Teacher

Driver

Chef

Match the words with the pictures

Red

Yellow

Blue

Green

Purple

Match the words with the pictures

Circle

Square

Rectangle

Hexagon

Octagon

Match the words with the pictures

Custard Apple

Guava

Blueberry

Jackfruit

Grapes

Match the words with the pictures

Carrot

Cabbage

Onion

Beetroot

Potato

Match the opposites

Big	Empty
Happy	Dirty
Hot	Hot
Fast	Dark
Light	Slow
Loud	New
Clean	Quiet
Full	Sad
Old	Cold

Fill the missing letters

T _ _ T L _

_ _ U S _

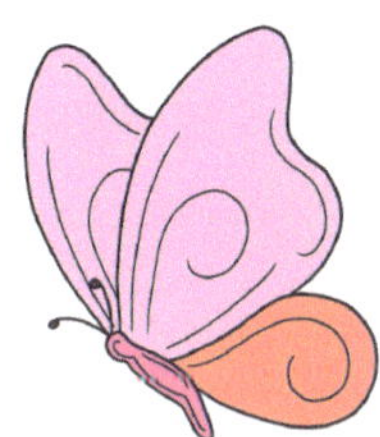

B _ T _ E R _ L Y

C _ _ U D

S _ N

Fill the missing letters

C O _ P U _ E _

B _ _ R

R A _ N B _ _

S O _ _ S

C _ O _ K

Find the odd one out

Find the odd one out

Match the animal and their younger ones

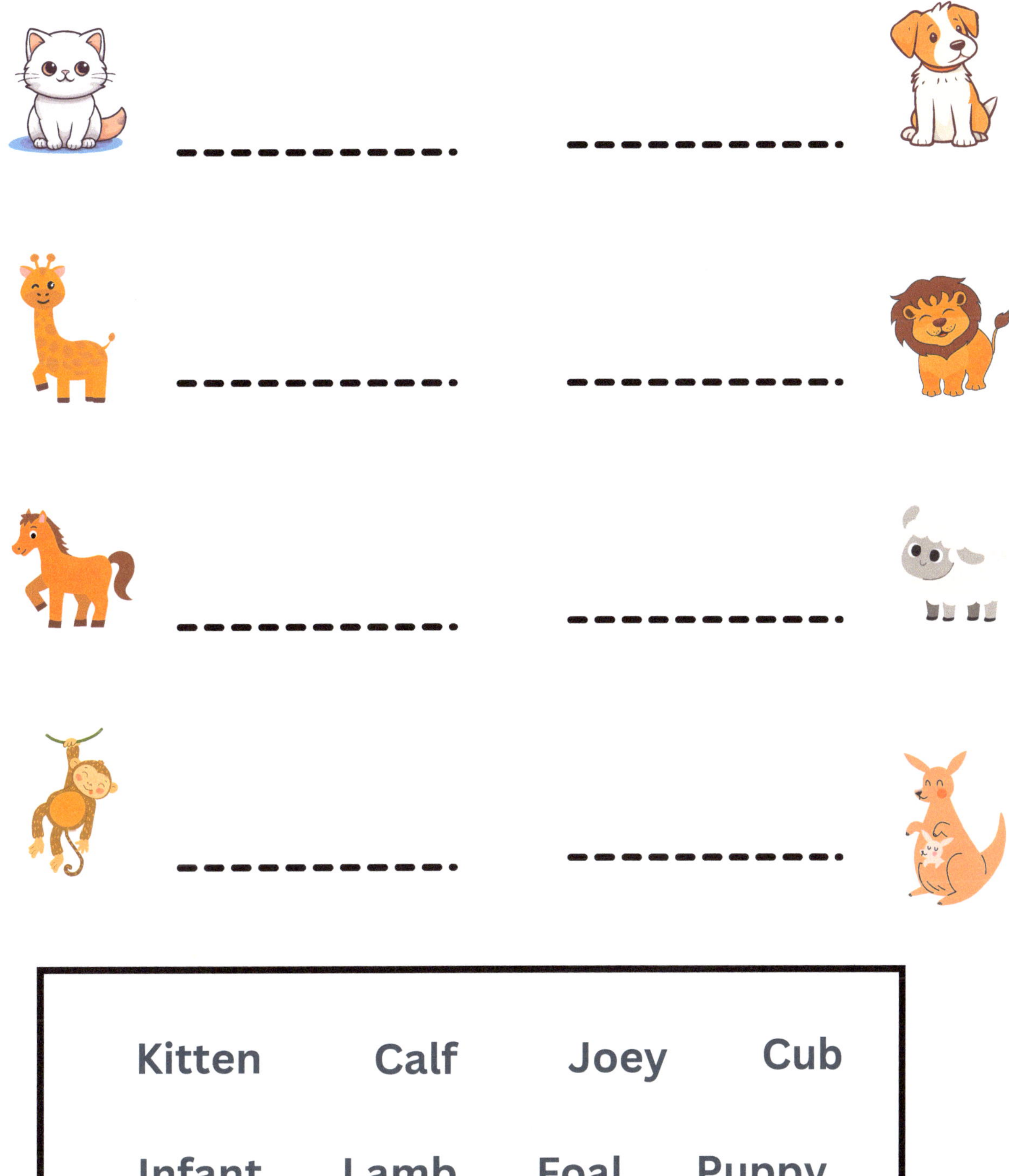

Kitten	Calf	Joey	Cub
Infant	Lamb	Foal	Puppy

Match the birds and their younger ones

Puffling	Duckling	Chick	Owlet
Eaglet	Peachick	Cygnet	Nestling

Complete the Homophones

S______ S______	F______ F______
D______ D______	S______ S______
B______ B______	N______ K______
B______ B______	H______ H______
P______ P______	W______ W______

Find the odd numbers

Colour the clouds with odd number in blue 

71 8 38 29

2 25 19

71 33 90 68

56 44

5 445

Find the even numbers

Colour the boxes with even number in red 

25	47	35	27	1	3	55
79	4	37	20	73	86	43
39	80	21	22	35	41	5
19	24	38	8	7	62	75
41	92	29	94	15	44	47
99	40	31	6	33	74	9
17	95	23	13	51	11	49

Write the word that you get after colouring

____

Circle the largest number

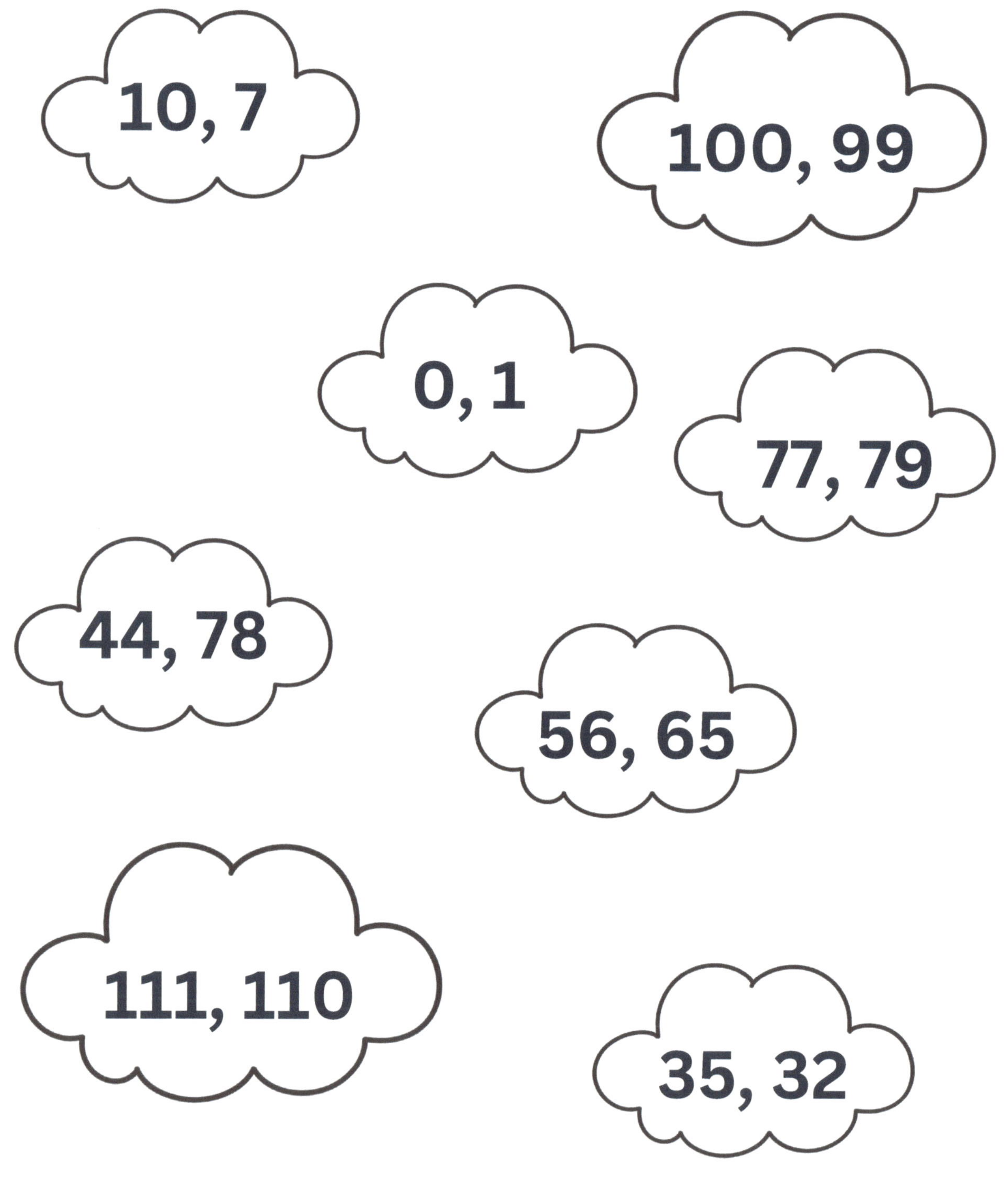

Complete the number pattern

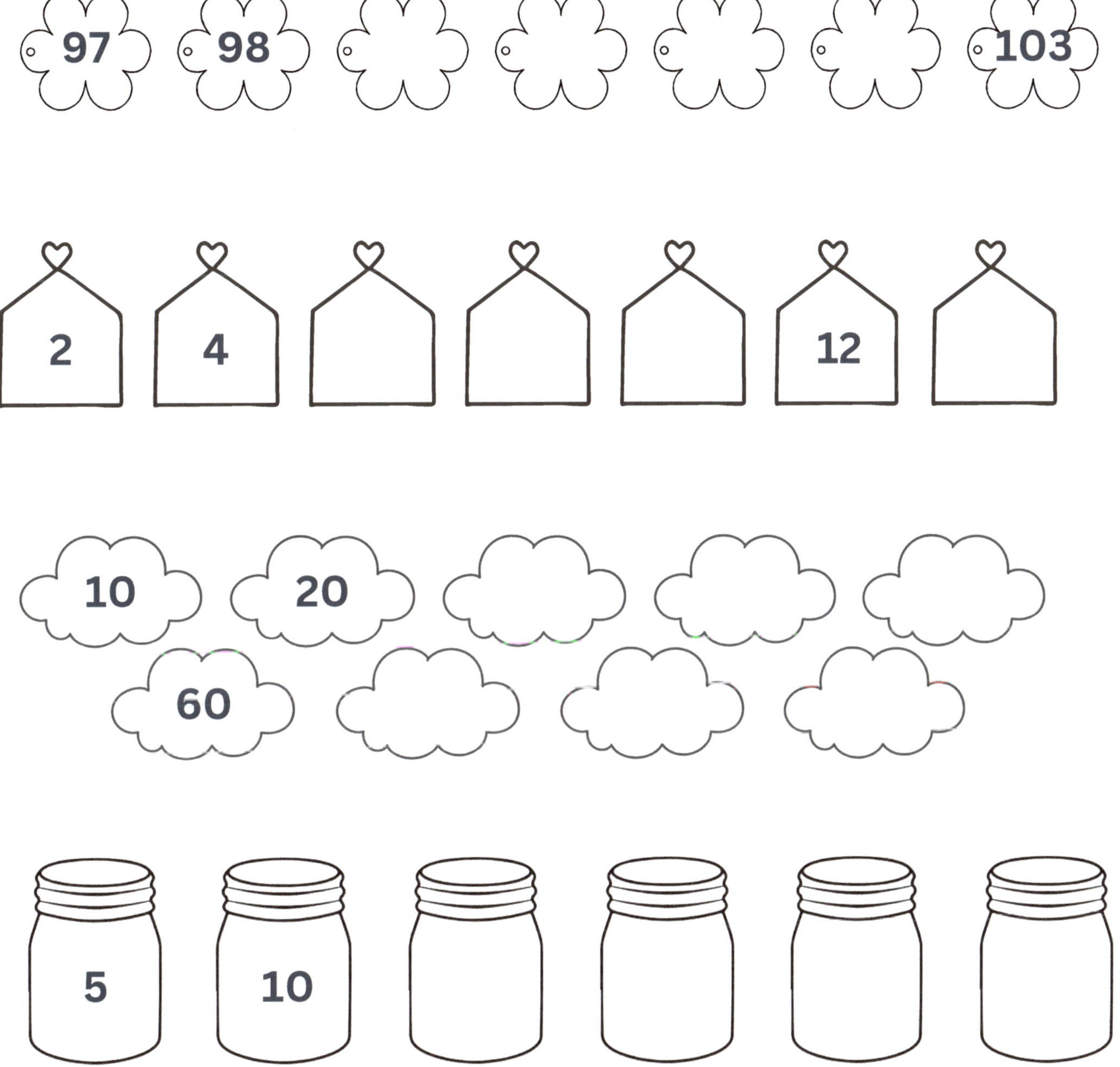

Complete the patterns

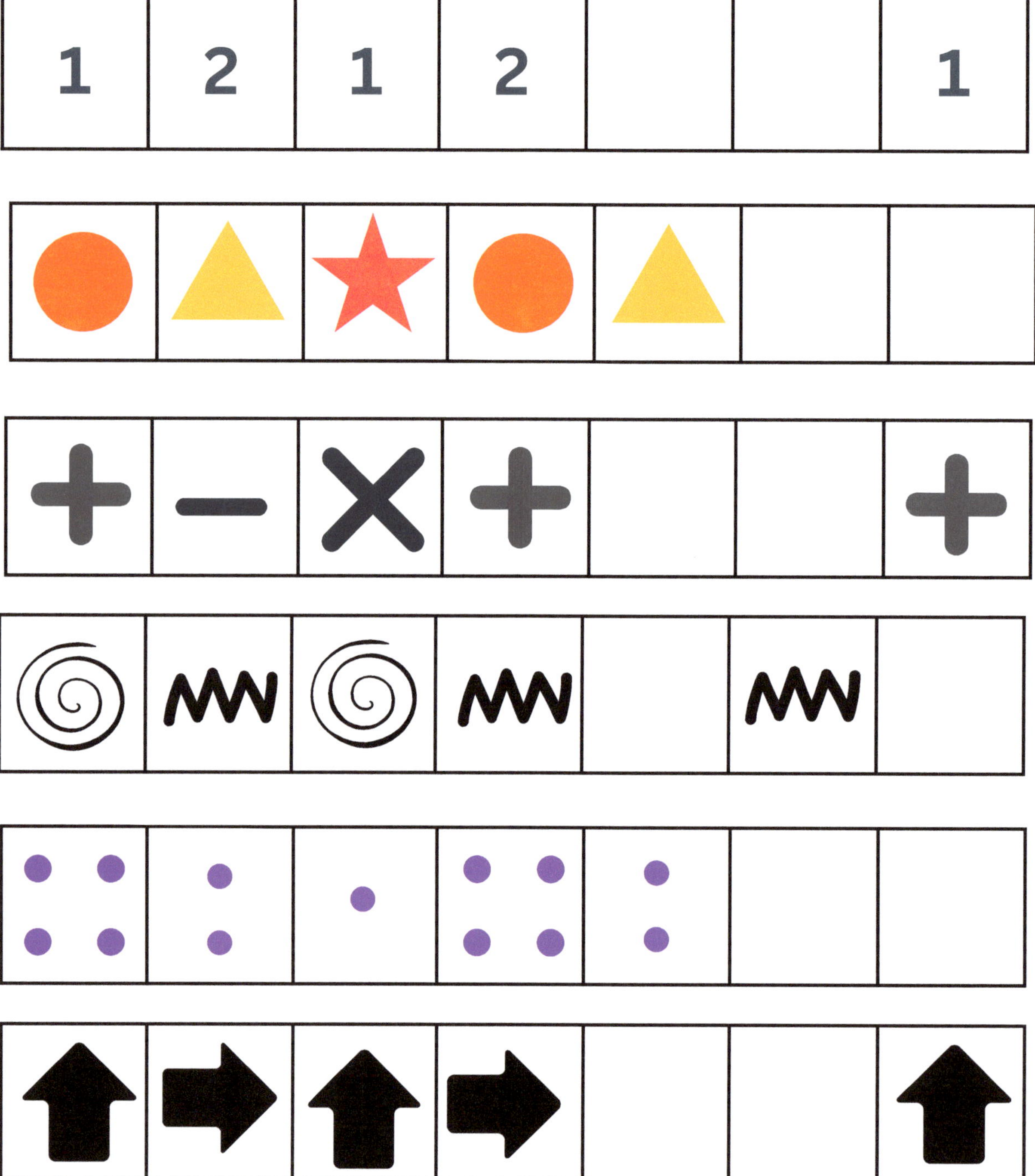

Help the baby elephant to reach its mother

Complete the calculations

	+		=
	-		=
	x	2	=
	÷	3	=
	+		=

www.ingramcontent.com/pod-product-compliance
Lightning Source LLC
LaVergne TN
LVHW071131160826
845679LV00005B/1249

* 9 7 9 8 8 9 6 9 9 7 1 5 3 *